Incredible Energy

Louise & Richard Spilsbury

Contents

Introduction	3
1 Energy Everywhere	4
2 Heat Energy	8
3 Sound and Light	12
4 Chemical Energy	16
5 Electricity	20
6 Fuels for Energy	24
7 Problems with Fuels	28
8 Saving Energy	32
Activities	36
Projects	52
Glossary	54
About *Read and Discover*	56

OXFORD
UNIVERSITY PRESS

Great Clarendon Street, Oxford OX2 6DP

Oxford University Press is a department of the University of Oxford. It furthers the University's objective of excellence in research, scholarship, and education by publishing worldwide in

Oxford New York

Auckland Cape Town Dar es Salaam Hong Kong Karachi
Kuala Lumpur Madrid Melbourne Mexico City Nairobi
New Delhi Shanghai Taipei Toronto

With offices in

Argentina Austria Brazil Chile Czech Republic France
Greece Guatemala Hungary Italy Japan Poland Portugal
Singapore South Korea Switzerland Thailand Turkey
Ukraine Vietnam

OXFORD and OXFORD ENGLISH are registered trade marks of Oxford University Press in the UK and in certain other countries

© Oxford University Press 2011

The moral rights of the author have been asserted

Database right Oxford University Press (maker)

First published 2011

2015 2014 2013 2012 2011
10 9 8 7 6 5 4 3 2 1

No unauthorized photocopying

All rights reserved. No part of this publication may be reproduced, stored in a retrieval system, or transmitted, in any form or by any means, without the prior permission in writing of Oxford University Press, or as expressly permitted by law, or under terms agreed with the appropriate reprographics rights organization. Enquiries concerning reproduction outside the scope of the above should be sent to the ELT Rights Department, Oxford University Press, at the address above

You must not circulate this book in any other binding or cover and you must impose this same condition on any acquirer

Any websites referred to in this publication are in the public domain and their addresses are provided by Oxford University Press for information only. Oxford University Press disclaims any responsibility for the content

ISBN: 978 0 19 464564 5

An Audio CD Pack containing this book and a CD is also available, ISBN 978 0 19 464604 8

The CD has a choice of American and British English recordings of the complete text.

An accompanying Activity Book is also available,
ISBN 978 0 19 464574 4

Printed in China

This book is printed on paper from certified and well-managed sources.

ACKNOWLEDGEMENTS

Illustrations by: Arlene Adams p.13; Kelly Kennedy pp.15, 21, 22, 31; Ian Moores pp.6, 9, 12, 24, 26, 30, 38; Dusan Pavlic/Beehive Illustration pp.44; Ben Shepard p.33 (wind machine).

The Publishers would also like to thank the following for their kind permission to reproduce photographs and other copyright material: Alamy p.6 (Martin Harvey); Corbis pp.17 (Rudy Sulgan), 19 (Ralph White/Terra); Getty Images pp.3 (Michael Grimm/Riser/pan), 7 (Mark Cosslett/National Geographic),10 (Michael Grimm/Riser), 14 (Mark Kolbe/Getty Images Sport), 16 (Joe Raedle/Getty Images News), 27 (Boris Starosta/Stock Illustration Source); Oxford University Press pp.3 (radio, bulb), 4, 8, 12, 18, 20; Photolibrary pp.5 (Eric Sanford/Ticket), 21 (Ian Murray/Loop Images), 22 (Andrea Sperling/Monsoon Images), 23 (Martin Leigh/Oxford Scientific), 28 (Ingo Kuzia/Intro/imagebroker.net); Reuters p.29 (Sheng Li); Science Photo Library pp.11 (Tony McConnell), 15 (Rosenfeld Images), 25 (Lowell Georgia), 31 (Patrick Landmann), 32 (Martin Bond), 33 (Volker Steger/wind farm), 34 (David Parker), 35 (Colin Cuthbert).

With thanks to Ann Fullick for science checking

Introduction

Energy is incredible because we use it for everything that we do. Energy can make things work, make things move, and make things happen. People use energy to work and to play. When people do things like cook food, listen to music, and use a lamp, they are using heat energy, sound energy, and light energy.

What types of energy can you see here?
What type of energy makes televisions and computers work?
What types of energy do you use every day?

Now read and discover more about incredible energy!

1 Energy Everywhere

Energy is everywhere and energy is in everything. We can't make energy and we can't destroy it. When we use energy to make something happen, we don't lose it. It becomes a different type of energy.

Converting Energy

One type of energy can be converted into another. For example, when we move, we use energy from the food that we eat. When runners use this energy to run fast in a race, some of it is converted into heat energy. That's why runners look and feel so hot at the end of a race!

Discover! When people run, only 25% of the energy in their legs is used to make them move. Most of it is converted into heat energy.

Kinetic Energy Making Sailing Boats Move

Different Types of Energy

There are many different types of energy, for example electrical energy and heat energy. Two important types of energy are kinetic energy and potential energy.

Kinetic energy is a type of energy that's moving. All things that move have kinetic energy. Wind is moving air. We use the kinetic energy in wind to fly kites and to sail boats.

Things that are not moving also have energy. Potential energy is stored energy. It's energy inside something that's waiting to be used. It's energy that has the potential to do work. We have potential energy stored in our bodies. When we run, some of this potential energy is converted into kinetic energy to make our legs move.

How Potential Energy Works

When we stretch a rubber band, we give it energy. The energy that we use to stretch the rubber band is stored inside it as potential energy. When we let go of the rubber band, it moves. When we stretch the rubber band more, it has more potential energy, and it can move more.

When we jump on a trampoline, this stretches the trampoline springs. This gives the springs potential energy. When the springs can't be stretched any more, this potential energy is converted into kinetic energy. The springs move back, and this throws us up into the air!

Jumping on a Trampoline

springs

From High to Low

Some things have potential energy because they are high up. When we lift a picture off the floor and put it on a wall, some of the energy that we use for lifting goes into the picture. If the picture falls off the wall, that potential energy is converted into kinetic energy. When something is very high up, it has a lot of potential energy. The water at the top of a high waterfall has a lot of potential energy. When it falls, it moves very fast because it has a lot of kinetic energy.

Discover!
Angel Falls in Venezuela is the highest waterfall in the world. The water falls almost 1 kilometer from top to bottom!

→ Go to pages 36–37 for activities.

Heat Energy

We use heat energy for many things. Heat energy makes our homes warm, cooks our food, and makes hot water that we can use for drinking and washing.

How We Get Heat Energy

We can get heat energy in different ways. Heat energy from the sun makes Earth warm. We can also get heat energy when we burn wood. When things move, some kinetic energy is converted into heat energy. Inside our body we make heat energy to keep us warm.

When heat is added to something, its temperature gets higher. When something has a high temperature it's very hot. Things are cold when they have less heat energy. When something is cold, it has a low temperature.

Inside Hot Things

Everything in the world is made of parts called atoms. Atoms join together to make molecules. Atoms and molecules are so small that we can't see them, but they are inside everything – rocks, water, air, and people.

When water is frozen, it becomes solid ice because it has very little heat energy. Molecules in ice are very near each other and they don't move very much. When heat energy is added to something, it makes the molecules inside move more. When heat energy is added to ice, molecules inside it move more. The ice melts and becomes liquid water again. If more heat is added to the water so that it boils, the molecules move so much that the water changes into a gas called steam.

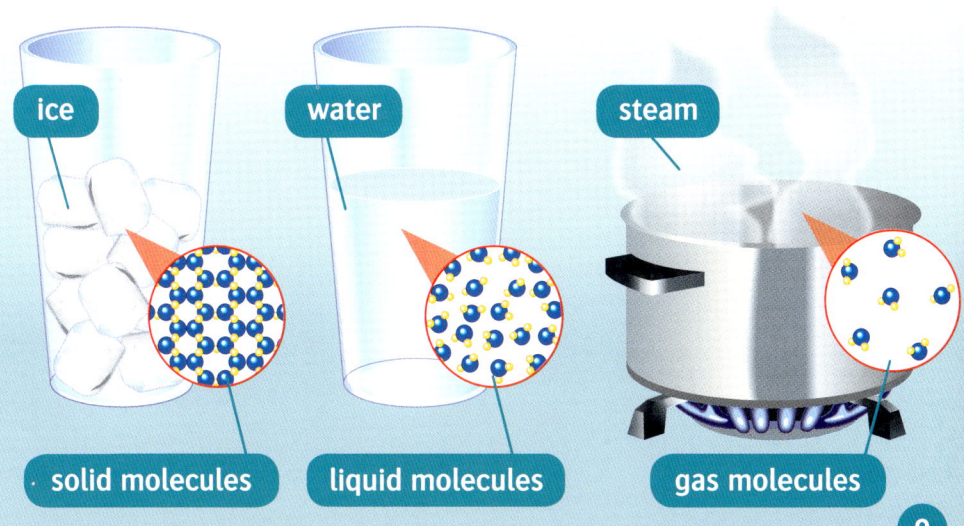

Water Molecules in Different Forms

ice — solid molecules

water — liquid molecules

steam — gas molecules

How Heat Energy Moves

Heat energy doesn't stay still. It moves from things that are warmer to things that are cooler. When heat moves between things that are touching, it's called conduction. Heat moves between two things until they are the same temperature.

Heat moves quickly and easily through some materials, like metal. For example, heat from a stove moves quickly through a metal pan to heat the food inside it. When we pick up a metal spoon from a table it feels cold because heat moves from our fingers into the spoon. Heat moves slowly through other materials, like wood. We use wooden spoons to stir food so that heat from the pan does not move into our hands.

A Metal Pan Heating Food

Heat Leaving a House

Insulators

To keep our homes warm when it's cold, we have to stop heat energy moving from the inside to the outside. In cold countries, people put insulators in the roofs of their homes. Insulators are materials that stop heat moving from warm places to cold places. Insulators in a roof stop heat moving from the rooms inside the home to the cold air outside.

Heat moves slowly through air, so air can be used as an insulator, too. When we wear a jacket in winter, the jacket holds air next to our body. The air stops heat leaving our body and so it helps to keep us warm.

→ Go to pages 38–39 for activities.

3 Sound and Light

Sound and light are types of energy that travel in the air. We use sound energy to hear, to listen to music, and to communicate by telephone. We use light energy from the sun to see during the day, and light from lamps to see when it's dark.

Sound

Sound happens when something vibrates. When we hit a drum, it vibrates and this makes the air around the drum vibrate, too. The vibrations of sound travel through the air in all directions. These movements are called sound waves. Sound waves are invisible – we can't see them. We hear the sound of the drum when the sound waves reach our ears.

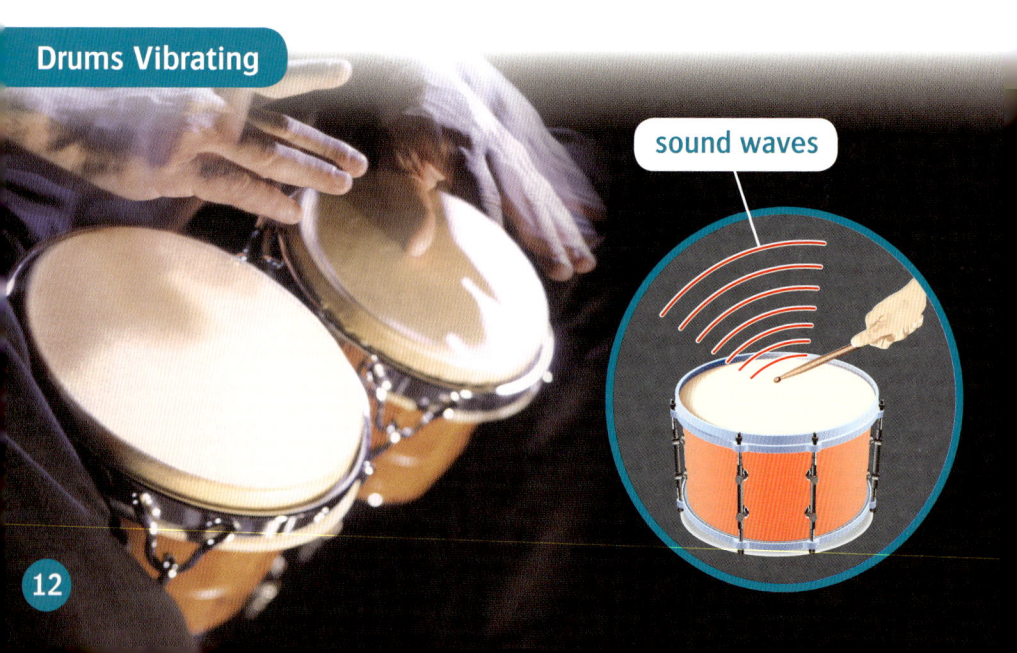

Drums Vibrating

sound waves

Radio Waves

Sounds lose energy and get weaker when they move. That's why we can only hear people speaking if they are near us. To send sounds from one place to another, sound waves are converted into radio waves. Radio waves are a type of energy that can travel a long distance through the air. Like sound waves, radio waves are invisible.

When you use a cell phone, the phone converts sound waves into radio waves. It sends the radio waves to a cell tower near you. The cell tower sends them to a base station that sends them on to a cell tower near the person you are calling. Their cell phone converts the radio waves back into sound waves so that they can hear you!

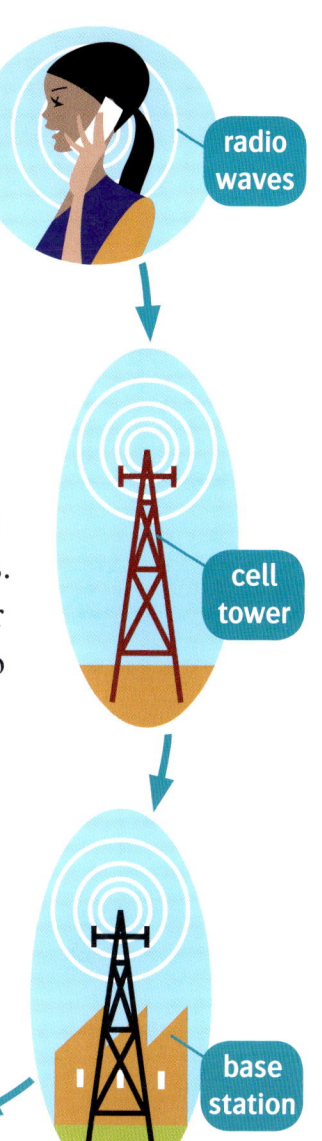

Light

When something is luminous, it gives off light. Lamps, candles, fires, televisions, and the sun are luminous. Light energy travels from luminous things in straight lines. Light can move through transparent things like air, water, and windows. It can't move through opaque things like walls, trees, or people.

Shadows happen when something opaque stops light moving through it. Shadows happen on the other side of an opaque thing, where light can't reach. For example, when we stand outside on a sunny day, we block the sunlight and we make a shadow. Some transparent materials can make a thin shadow because they stop some light.

Making Shadows

shadow

A Laser Cutting Metal

Lasers

A laser is a type of light that we get from machines. It's a very thin beam of light that has a lot of light energy and heat energy. Lasers have more energy than sunlight! We use lasers in many machines, like CD players and DVD players. Lasers have so much energy that some factories use them to cut through metal, and doctors use lasers to operate on some parts of the body, like eyes.

Discover!

In clothes factories, people use lasers to cut through hundreds of pieces of fabric at the same time.

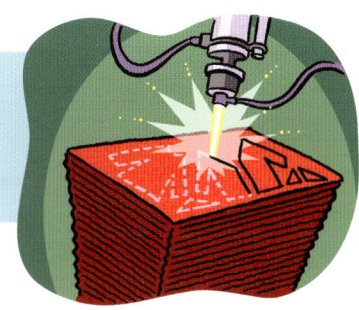

→ Go to pages 40–41 for activities.

Chemical Energy

Chemical energy is a type of potential energy. Wood and gasoline have chemical energy. Chemical energy is very useful because we can convert it into many other types of energy.

Using Chemical Energy

When a material has chemical energy, we call this material fuel. Fuels like wood and gasoline have a lot of chemical energy. When we burn gasoline in a car engine, chemical energy from the fuel is converted into kinetic energy that makes the car move. When we burn wood in a fire, chemical energy is converted into heat energy to keep us warm.

Discover!
The engine in a rocket converts chemical energy from fuel into kinetic energy to send the rocket into space!

Fireworks

Inside a firework there are powders that use chemical energy in different ways. When we burn a firework, these different types of chemical energy are converted into an amazing, colorful display of kinetic energy, light energy, and sound energy!

The first thing that burns in a firework is fuel. This gives us the kinetic energy that sends the firework up into the sky. Then, different metals start to burn and they make sparks of different colors. For example, when copper burns it makes blue sparks. Some chemicals inside the firework make loud sounds when they burn.

Food Energy

Food has chemical energy, too. Our body converts the chemical energy in our food into chemical energy that we can use to live, to move, and to grow. The chemical energy in our food, and in the food that other animals eat, comes from plants.

Food Chains

Plants convert light energy from the sun into chemical energy that they can use as food. Plants also store chemical energy.

When an animal, like a gazelle, eats plants, it uses some of the chemical energy from the plant. When a lion eats a gazelle, it uses some of the chemical energy from the gazelle's body. When energy from food moves from one living thing to another like this, it's called a food chain.

A Food Chain

plants → gazelle → lion

Chemicals in the Ocean

Most food chains start with energy from the sun, but some food chains in the ocean start with a different type of energy. The rock under deep oceans is very, very hot. When water goes underground through small holes, the rock makes the water as hot as the inside of a pizza oven. The hot water dissolves some of the chemicals in the rock. So the chemicals become part of the water. When water with chemicals dissolved in it comes out of the rock, living things called bacteria feed on the chemicals. Other animals in the ocean feed on the bacteria.

Discover! Deep in the ocean, some bacteria live inside the bodies of giant worms that can be 3 meters long! The bacteria make food for the worms.

worms

→ Go to pages 42–43 for activities.

 Electricity

How often do you use televisions, lights, and computers? Without electricity, these and many other machines can't work! Electricity is a very useful type of energy that gives us heat energy, light energy, sound energy, and kinetic energy.

A Flash of Lightning

What Is Electricity?

Inside atoms there are parts called electrons. Electrons can move from one atom to another, and when they do this they make electricity.

Lightning is a type of electricity. It happens when the wind makes atoms of ice inside clouds move around and crash into each other. Electrons move quickly from one atom to another, and we see this movement of electricity as a flash of lightning.

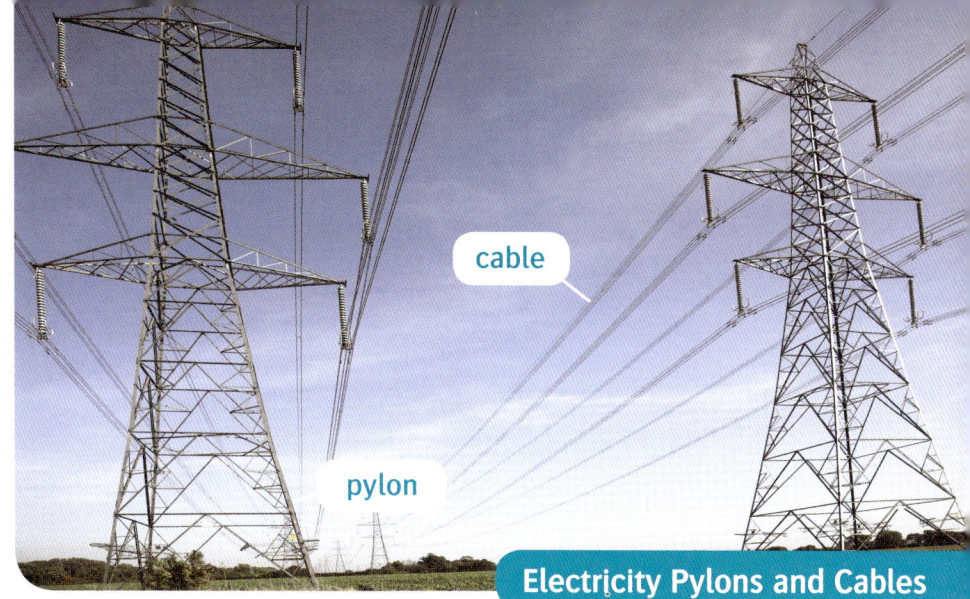

Electricity Pylons and Cables

How Electricity Moves

Power stations are factories that make electricity. The electricity goes through cables and pylons to our homes. This electricity makes the machines in our homes work.

Some materials are called conductors – electricity can move easily through these materials. Most metals, like copper and gold, are good conductors. This is why electricity cables are made of metal. Other materials, like rubber and air, are called insulators – electricity can't move easily through these materials.

Discover! Some animals are dangerous because they make their own electricity. Electric eels store electricity in their body and use it to kill other fish!

A Light Bulb

wire

Using Electricity

Electricity gives us different types of energy. In a toaster, electricity is used to make heat energy to cook bread. Wires inside a toaster are made from a type of metal that slows down the electricity so that some of its energy is converted into heat.

In a hairdryer, electric wires give us heat energy and then electricity turns a fan. The fan uses kinetic energy to push the heat out of the hairdryer so that we can dry our hair.

In many electric lamps, electricity moves slowly through a thin, curly wire inside a light bulb. This makes the wire so hot that it becomes white, and it glows to give us light.

Discover! Most of the electricity that moves through the wire in a light bulb is converted into heat, not light!

Using Batteries

Some machines, like calculators and music players, use batteries for their electrical energy. Batteries only give us small amounts of electricity, but they are useful because they can store electricity to use in machines that we take with us when we travel around. Small batteries are useful in small machines like watches. Bigger batteries have more potential energy and we can use them in machines like flashlights. Some machines need two or more batteries.

Batteries store chemical energy. The chemical energy is converted into electricity when we turn on a machine. The chemicals inside a battery are dangerous, so never play with a battery or open a battery.

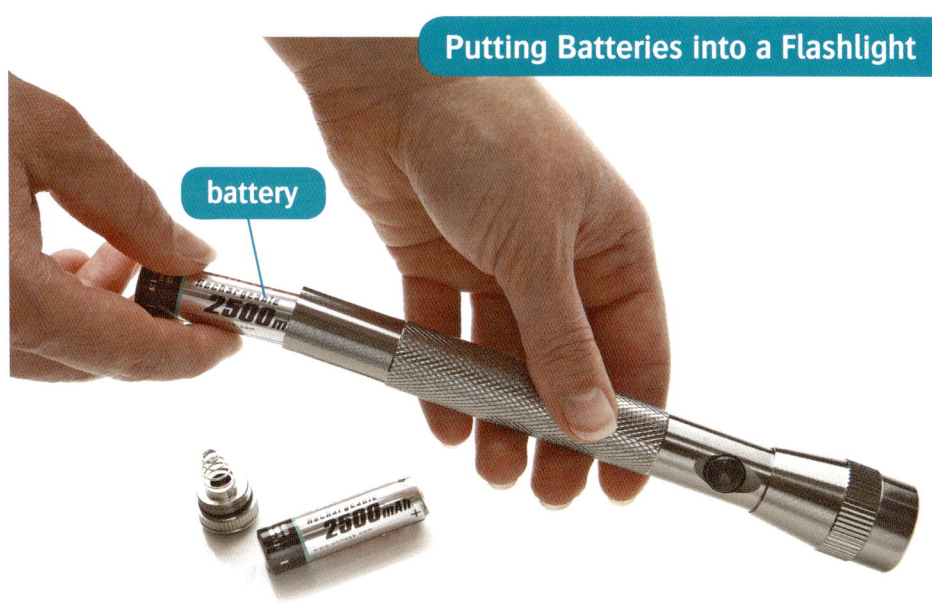

Putting Batteries into a Flashlight

battery

→ Go to pages 44–45 for activities.

6 Fuels for Energy

Coal, oil, and gas are fossil fuels. We use fossil fuels and nuclear fuels to make electricity. We use fossil fuels to heat homes and to power cars, buses, and trucks.

Fossil Fuels

Fossil fuels are made from plants and animals that lived on Earth millions of years ago. Coal was made like this. When giant plants in ancient jungles died, they sank into mud. Slowly, over millions of years, the mud became hard and changed into rock. The heavy rock pressed down on the plants, and heat from inside Earth helped to change the plants into black coal. Oil and gas were also made like this, but they come from animals that lived in ancient oceans.

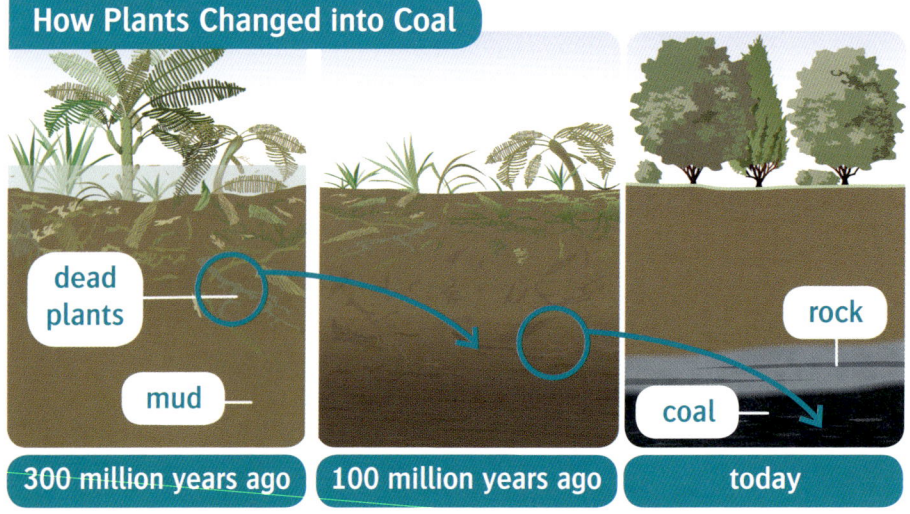

How Plants Changed into Coal

dead plants | mud — 300 million years ago | 100 million years ago | rock | coal — today

Getting Coal

Miners are people who get coal from under the ground. They use machines to cut holes and tunnels in the ground. Then they cut pieces of coal out of the rock from under the ground. Trucks and trains take coal to power stations or to people's homes, where the coal is burned to give us heat.

Getting Oil and Gas

People get oil from oil rigs in the ocean, and they get gas and more oil from wells on land. The oil and gas move through long pipes to where people need it. People mostly use gas for heating and cooking. They usually use oil to make gasoline and to make new chemicals.

Discover!
One of the longest gas pipes in the ocean goes 1,200 kilometers from Norway to the United Kingdom.

Gas Pipes, USA

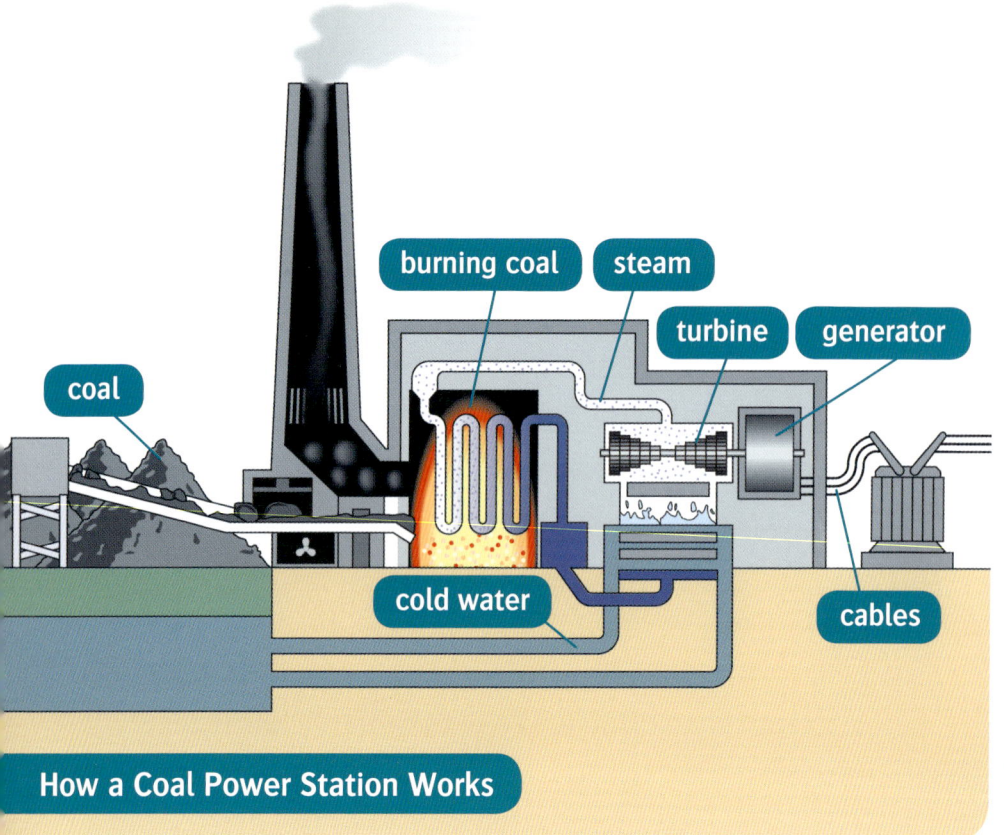

How a Coal Power Station Works

Fossil Fuels for Electricity

Most large power stations use the chemical energy in coal to make electricity. In a coal power station, people use heat energy from burning coal to boil water. The boiling water makes steam that has lots of kinetic energy. The steam turns a turbine. The turbine turns a generator and this makes electricity. Cold water then cools the steam and converts it back into water. Some water is heated up again by burning more coal to make more steam. The electricity moves through cables to our homes and other buildings where we can use it.

Nuclear Energy

Nuclear energy doesn't come from fossil fuels. It's a different type of energy. Nuclear fuel is a metal called uranium. We get nuclear energy when atoms inside uranium are broken. Every atom has a part called the nucleus, and this is where nuclear energy is. When a uranium atom breaks open, the energy comes out as heat. When many atoms break open at the same time, large amounts of heat are made.

Heat from nuclear energy is used to make steam that turns turbines and generators in a nuclear power station. In nuclear submarines, the steam turns propellers that move the submarine forward.

A Nuclear Submarine

propeller

→ Go to pages 46–47 for activities.

 Problems with Fuels

About 75% of the energy that people use for power stations and vehicles around the world is made from fossil fuels. Fossil fuels and nuclear fuels are very useful, but there are problems with using both of them.

Using Earth's Coal

Non-Renewable Fuels

One problem with fossil fuels is that they are non-renewable. Fossil fuels are made from plants and animals that lived millions of years ago. When we have used all the fossil fuels that are on Earth now, there will not be any more. Some scientists say that oil will run out in 40 to 70 years, and gas in 50 to 150 years. Coal will run out in about 1,000 years.

Dirty Air

When fossil fuels are burned, they make different gases that make the air dirty. This is called air pollution. Air pollution is bad for plants, animals, and people.

Power stations and vehicles make air pollution. When gasoline is burned in cars and other vehicles, people who are walking or riding bicycles in the streets sometimes start to cough. The problem is worse in cities, where there are many cars. In some cities you can see the air is dirty. Some people wear a mask over their face so that they don't breathe the pollution.

Discover! There are 700 million cars in the world. There may be 1,400 million in 30 years!

Air Pollution in City Streets

mask

How Greenhouse Gases Work

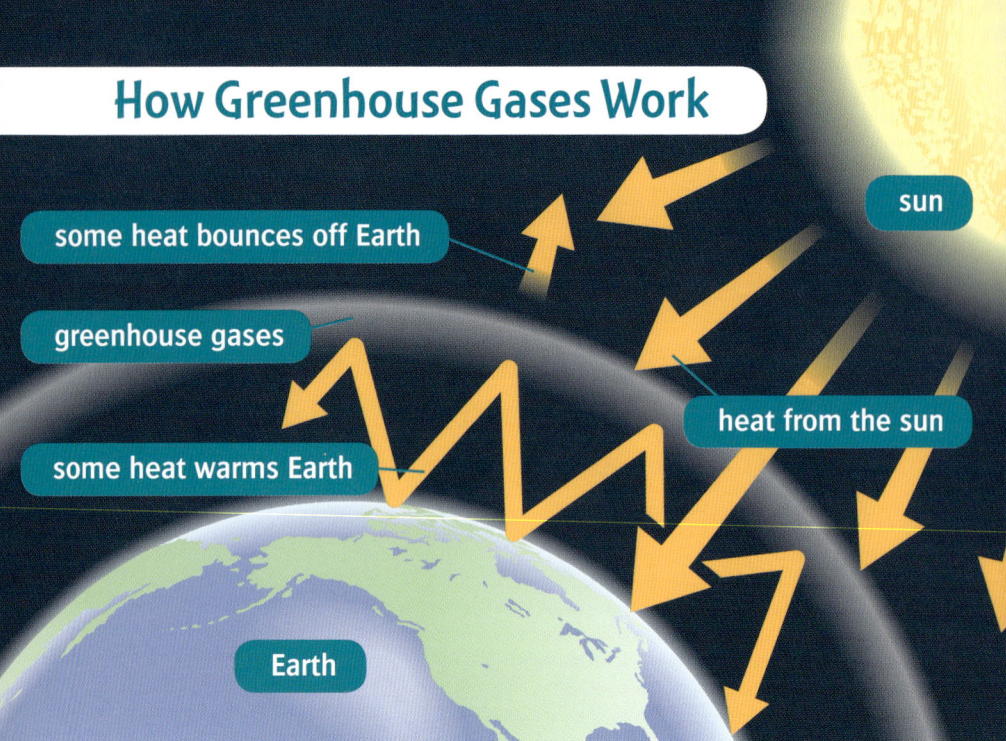

Greenhouse gases are a mixture of gases in the air around Earth. When heat from the sun warms Earth, some of it bounces off Earth and goes back into space. Greenhouse gases stop some of this heat going back into space.

Greenhouse gases are useful because they store the heat and they keep Earth warm. Without greenhouse gases, Earth would be so cold that we would not be able to live here!

Greenhouse Gas Problems

When lots of fossil fuels are burned, they put too many greenhouses gases into the air. This makes it warmer on Earth and it can change the world's climate. This is called global warming.

Many scientists think that global warming has started forest fires, has created more floods, and is melting glaciers and ice in the Arctic and Antarctic.

Discover! If polar bears in the Arctic don't have ice to climb onto, they could die.

Nuclear Problems

The biggest problem with nuclear fuel is that after uranium has been used, it makes dangerous radioactive waste. The radioactive waste stays dangerous for hundreds of years so it has to be stored very, very carefully. The radioactive waste is invisible, but it's very dangerous and it can kill living things.

Storing Radioactive Waste

→ Go to pages 48–49 for activities.

8 Saving Energy

There are problems with fossil fuels and nuclear fuels, and we need to use more renewable energy. Renewable energy comes from things like wind, water, and sunlight. These are types of energy that will not run out.

Solar Panels Making Electricity

solar panels

Solar Energy

People use the sun's energy, or solar energy, to heat water and to make electricity. In some homes, solar panels use the sun to heat water. The panels take heat from the sun and then they heat the water in pipes. Some types of solar panel have photovoltaic cells inside. The photovoltaic cells convert sunlight into electricity. They can be used in small machines like laptops, or on a roof to make electricity. Many photovoltaic cells together can make electricity for thousands of people.

Wind Energy

Wind is moving air. To catch wind energy, people build wind turbines in windy places, like high hills or near beaches. Wind turbines are tall and they have three or four blades at the top. The blades turn like a propeller when the wind blows on them. The blades then turn a generator inside the wind turbine to create electricity. When many wind turbines are built together to make a lot of electricity, this is called a wind farm.

A Wind Farm

blade

wind turbine

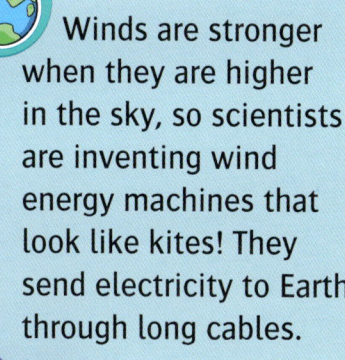

cable

Discover! Winds are stronger when they are higher in the sky, so scientists are inventing wind energy machines that look like kites! They send electricity to Earth through long cables.

Energy from Water

People can use the kinetic energy of moving water to make electricity. For example, water that moves down mountains moves very quickly and so it has a lot of kinetic energy. In a hydroelectric power station, this water moves quickly into pipes, which push it through turbines. The water turns turbines that turn generators to make electricity.

Some hydroelectric power stations are next to rivers. A large wall called a dam holds the water so it becomes a store of potential energy. When the water stored behind a dam is pushed through pipes and turbines, the potential energy is converted into kinetic energy that can be used to make electricity.

The Hoover Dam is one of the biggest hydroelectric power stations in the USA. It makes electricity for about 1.3 million people.

A Bicycle Park, the Netherlands

What Can We Do?

We can all help to save energy. We can use fewer fossil fuels every day by changing some of the things that we do. For example, we can save oil by walking, riding bicycles, sharing rides to school, or traveling by bus instead of making all our journeys by car. This will also reduce the amount of air pollution and greenhouse gases that go into the air. We can use less electricity by turning off lights and electric machines when we aren't using them.

In the future, there will be more people on Earth and we will need more electricity and more energy for our vehicles. What will you do to help to save energy for the future?

➜ Go to pages 50–51 for activities.

1 Energy Everywhere

← Read pages 4–7.

1 Write *true* or *false*.

1 When we use energy, we lose it. _false_

2 When we use energy, it becomes a different type of energy. _____

3 When we move, we use energy from the food that we eat. _____

4 When runners run, some of their energy is converted into light energy. _____

2 Complete the sentences.

sailing boats   stored   ~~energy~~   Potential   Wind   kinetic

1 There are many different types of _energy_.

2 All things that move have _____ energy.

3 _____ has kinetic energy.

4 Kinetic energy makes _____ move.

5 _____ energy is stored energy.

6 When we run, potential energy that's _____ in our body is converted into kinetic energy.

3 Order the words.

1 stretch a / we give it energy. / When we / rubber band,

   When we stretch a rubber band, we give it energy.

2 jump on a / When we / its springs. / this stretches / trampoline,

   _____

3 potential energy. / the springs / When we stretch / this gives / a trampoline

   _____

4 When springs / is converted into kinetic energy. / potential energy / can't be stretched any more,

   _____

4 Circle the correct words.

1 Some things have **(potential)** / **kinetic** energy because they are high up.

2 When you lift something off the floor, some of the **energy** / **time** that you use goes into it.

3 When something falls, potential energy is converted into **kinetic** / **heat** energy.

4 When something is very high up, it has a lot of **potential** / **kinetic** energy.

5 Water in a high waterfall moves fast because it has a lot of **potential** / **kinetic** energy.

2 Heat Energy

← Read pages 8–11.

1 Match.

1 Heat energy from the sun — makes Earth warm.
2 Inside our body, heat energy — keeps us warm.
3 We can use heat energy to — make our homes warm.
4 When heat is added to something — its temperature gets higher.
5 When something is cold — it has a low temperature.

2 Circle the correct words.

1 Everything in the world is made of parts called **atoms** / **air**.

2 Atoms join together to make **molecules** / **rocks**.

3 Atoms and molecules are very **big** / **small**.

4 When heat energy is added to something, it makes the molecules inside move **more** / **less**.

3 Match. Then write the words.

~~liquid molecules~~
solid molecules
gas molecules

1 _____

2 _____

3 liquid molecules

4 Complete the sentences.

> conduction   temperature   wood   cooler   materials

1 Heat energy moves from things that are warmer to things that are _____ .

2 When heat moves between things that are touching, it's called _____ .

3 Heat moves between two things until they are the same _____ .

4 Heat moves quickly through _____ like metal.

5 Heat moves slowly through materials like _____ .

5 Answer the questions.

1 What do we have to do to keep our homes warm when it's cold?
   We have to stop heat moving from the inside to the outside.

2 What do insulators do?
   _____

3 Why can we use air as an insulator?
   _____

4 How do jackets help to keep us warm in winter?
   _____

3 Sound and Light

← Read pages 12–15.

~~windows~~   walls   water
trees   doors   air

1 Complete the chart.

Things that are transparent:	Things that are opaque:
windows	

2 Order the words.

1 that travel in the air. / are types of energy / Sound and light

_____

2 when something / Sound happens / vibrates.

_____

3 it makes the air / around the drum vibrate, too. / When a drum vibrates,

_____

4 travel through the air / The vibrations / in all directions. / of sound

_____

5 are called / in the air / The vibrations / sound waves. / of sound

_____

3 Correct the sentences.

1 Sounds get more energy and get stronger when they move.

<u>Sounds lose energy and get weaker when they move.</u>

2 To send sounds from one place to another, light waves are converted into radio waves.

_____

3 Radio waves are visible. We can see them.

_____

4 Cell phones convert radio waves back into sound waves so that we can see the sounds.

_____

4 Write *true* or *false*.

1 When something is luminous, it gives off light. _____

2 Lamps, candles, and fires are not luminous. _____

3 Shadows happen when something opaque stops light moving through it. _____

4 A laser is a type of light that we get from the sun. _____

5 A laser beam has very little energy. _____

6 Doctors use lasers to operate on some parts of the body. _____

5 Write about sounds that you like.

_____

_____

_____

4 Chemical Energy

← Read pages 16–19.

1 Complete the puzzle. Then write the secret word.

1. Materials that have chemical energy are called __ .
2. Chemical energy is a type of __ energy.
3. Wood and gasoline have a lot of chemical __
4. In a car engine, chemical energy from fuel is converted into __ energy.
5. Inside a firework there are __ that use chemical energy in different ways.
6. Fireworks convert chemical energy into kinetic energy, light energy, and __ energy.
7. The __ thing that burns in a firework is fuel.
8. When metals in a firework burn, they make __ of different colors.
9. Some __ inside fireworks make loud sounds when they are burned.

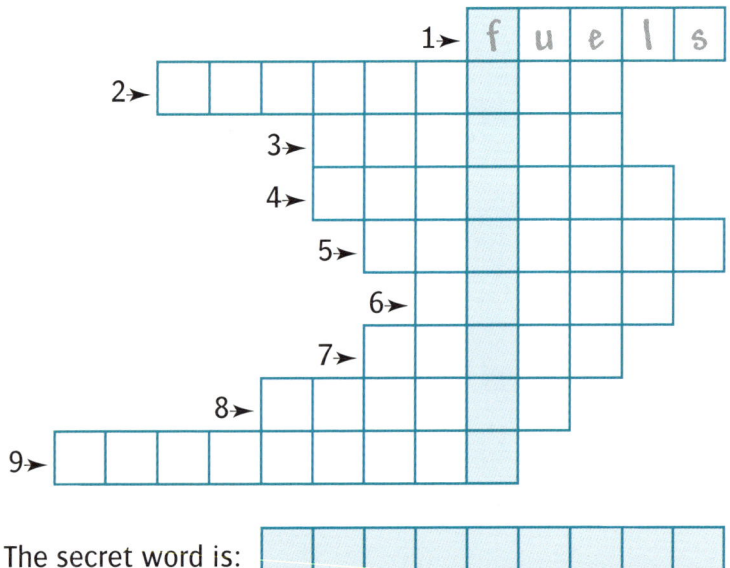

1. f u e l s

The secret word is:

2 Match. Then write the sentences.

We use chemical energy from food

Plants convert light energy

Plants store

Animals eat plants to use some

In food chains, energy from food

chemical energy.

from the sun into chemical energy.

of the chemical energy from the plant.

moves from one living thing to another.

to live, to move, and to grow.

1 We use chemical energy from food to live, to move, and to grow.

2 _____

3 _____

4 _____

5 _____

3 Complete the sentences.

energy   sun   dissolves   chemicals

1 Most living things need energy from the _____ .

2 Some food chains in the oceans start with a different type of _____ .

3 Hot water _____ some of the chemicals in rock under deep oceans.

4 Living things called bacteria feed on the _____ .

5 Electricity

← Read pages 20–23.

light energy   heat energy
kinetic energy   sound energy

1 Write the type of energy.

1 _____

2 _____

3 _____

4 _____

2 Complete the sentences.

movement   electrons   lightning   electricity

1 Inside atoms there are parts called _____ .

2 When electrons move from one atom to another, they make _____ .

3 One type of electricity is _____ .

4 A flash of lightning is the _____ of electricity.

3 Write *true* or *false*.

1 Power stations are factories that make electricity. _____

2 Electricity can't move easily through materials called conductors. _____

3 Most metals are bad conductors. _____

4 Electricity cables are made of metal. _____

5 Electricity can't move easily through materials called insulators. _____

4 Order the words.

1 is used / In a toaster, / to cook bread. / electricity

_____

2 slow down electricity / is converted / Metal wires / so that / some of its energy / in a toaster / into heat.

_____

3 give us heat. / electric wires / In a hairdryer,

_____

4 a hairdryer / Electricity turns / to dry hair. / to push heat / out of / a fan

_____

5 a wire / so hot / white and glows. / electricity makes / In a lamp, / that it becomes

_____

5 Answer the questions.

1 What do small machines like calculators use for their electrical energy?

_____

2 Why are batteries useful?

_____

3 When is the chemical energy in a battery converted into electricity?

_____

4 Why shouldn't you play with a battery or open a battery?

_____

6 Fuels for Energy

← Read pages 24–27.

1 Find and write the words.

f	i	o	c	c	e	a	r	t	h
u	x	i	a	n	c	i	e	n	t
e	t	l	t	a	b	y	h	e	c
l	n	e	m	u	d	g	e	s	e
s	q	w	c	d	x	e	a	o	m
l	f	c	o	a	l	n	t	w	l
b	p	l	a	n	t	s	n	g	s
l	u	n	a	n	i	m	a	l	s
f	u	a	t	o	i	r	a	t	i
t	x	d	j	u	n	g	l	e	s

1 _fuels_
2 c_____
3 o_____
4 a_____
5 j_____
6 e_____
7 h_____
8 m_____
9 a_____
10 p_____

2 Circle the correct words.

1 Coal, oil, and **gas** / **water** are fossil fuels.

2 Coal is made from **plants** / **animals** that lived millions of years ago.

3 Oil and gas come from animals that lived in ancient **forests** / **oceans**.

4 People who collect coal are called **miners** / **doctors**.

5 People cut coal out of the rock under the **ground** / **ocean**.

6 People **mostly** / **never** use gas for heating and cooking.

7 People usually use **oil** / **coal** in cars and other vehicles.

3 Order the words. Then answer the questions.

1 What do / electricity? / large power stations / use to make

_____

_____

2 coal power station? / burn coal / in a / Why do people

_____

_____

3 have? / does steam / of energy / What type / from boiling water

_____

_____

4 power station, / In a / steam turn? / what does

_____

_____

5 make electricity? / help to / a turbine / How does

_____

_____

4 Write *true* or *false*.

1 We get nuclear energy when atoms inside uranium are joined. _____

2 Nuclear fuel is a metal called uranium. _____

3 Nuclear energy is in the nucleus of an atom. _____

4 When a fuel atom breaks open, the energy comes out as heat. _____

7 Problems with Fuels

← Read pages 28–31.

1 Write sentences with these words.

> ~~fossil fuels~~   non-renewable   oil   gas

1 _Fossil fuels are made from plants and animals that lived millions of years ago._

2 _____

3 _____

4 _____

2 Correct the sentences.

1 Fossil fuels make different gases that make the air clean.

_____

2 Air pollution is good for plants, animals, and people.

_____

3 Power stations and vehicles stop air pollution.

_____

4 Air pollution is worse in cities where there are few cars.

_____

5 In some cities, people wear a mask over their bicycle.

_____

3 Write the sentences in order.

Greenhouses gases store — heat and keep Earth warm.
Greenhouses gases stop — some heat going back into space.
Some heat bounces off Earth — and goes back into space.
Heat from the sun — warms Earth.

How greenhouse gases keep Earth warm:

1 Heat from the sun warms Earth.
2 _____
3 _____
4 _____

4 Complete the sentences.

fires   uranium   warming   ice   invisible   air   climate

1 Burning fossil fuels puts more greenhouses gases into the _____ .

2 More greenhouses gases can change the world's _____ .

3 This is called global _____ .

4 In some countries, global warming has started forest _____ .

5 The _____ is melting at the Arctic and Antarctic.

6 After _____ has been used, it makes radioactive waste.

7 Radioactive waste is _____ .

49

8 Saving Energy

← Read pages 32–35.

1 Match.

1 We need to use fewer
2 Renewable energy comes
3 Renewable energy
4 People use solar energy
5 Solar panels in a roof use
6 Photovoltaic cells

will not run out.
to heat water and to make electricity.
heat from the sun to warm water.
convert sunlight into electricity.
fossil fuels.
from wind, water, and sunlight.

2 Complete the sentences.

propeller   blades   air   tall   generator   turbines

1 Wind is moving _____ .

2 To catch wind energy, people build wind _____ in windy places.

3 Wind turbines are _____ .

4 Wind turbines have three or four _____ at the top.

5 The blades turn like a _____ when the wind blows on them.

6 The blades turn a _____ inside the wind turbine to create electricity.

3 Answer the questions.

1 What type of energy does moving water have?
   _____

2 What happens in a hydroelectric power station?
   _____

3 What does a dam do?
   _____

4 What happens when water behind a dam is pushed through turbines?
   _____

5 How much electricity does the Hoover Dam make?
   _____

4 Write about the things you do to save energy. What other things could you do to save energy for the future?

_____

_____

_____

_____

_____

_____

_____

Project 1 An Energy Survey

1 Write notes about the electricity that you use.

What machine do you use?	What do you use it for?	How long do you use it for?

2 Write about your results.

3 Display your results.

Project 2 — An Energy Poster

1. Design a poster about saving energy. Write notes.

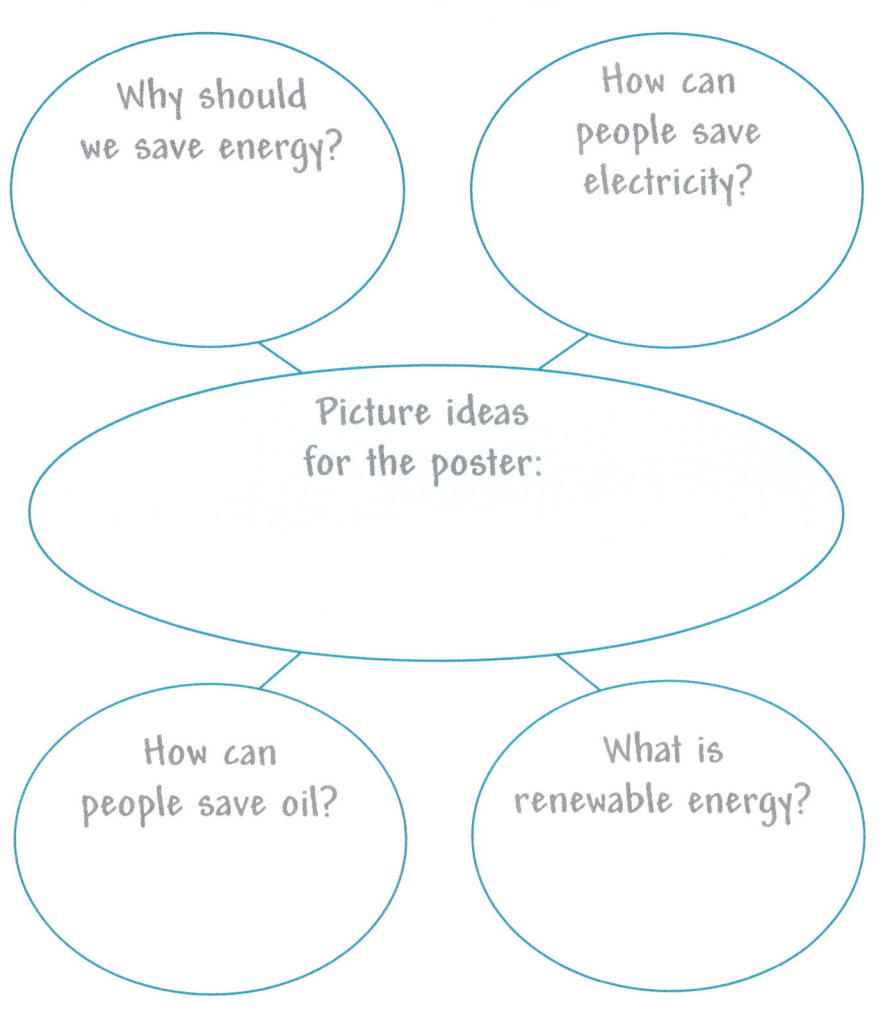

- Why should we save energy?
- How can people save electricity?
- Picture ideas for the poster:
- How can people save oil?
- What is renewable energy?

2. Make a poster. Write sentences and add pictures to decorate your poster.

3. Display your poster.

Glossary

Here are some words used in this book, and you can check what they mean. Use a dictionary to check other new words.

air pollution when the air around us is made dirty
atom everything is made of parts called atoms, but atoms are so small that we can't see them
bacteria very simple living things
battery (*plural* **batteries**) something that goes inside machines to make them work
beam a straight line of light
boil to heat a liquid like water until it's so hot that it changes into steam
bulb the part of an electric lamp that produces light
burn to make flames and heat
cable a metal rope that electricity moves through
change to become different
chemical a solid or liquid that's made by chemistry; made from chemicals
climate the usual type of weather in a country
coal a hard, black fossil fuel
conduction the way that heat moves between things that are touching
conductor a material that electricity can move through
convert to become different; to make something different
cool to become colder; to make something colder
copper a soft, orange or yellow metal
deep going a long way down
destroy to break something or to make it bad or weak
die to stop living
display something in a place where people can see it easily
dissolve to mix with water and become part of it
distance the space between two places
electricity a type of energy
electron a very small part of an atom
energy we need energy to move and grow, and machines need energy to work
engine a machine that produces energy
fabric a soft material
fan a machine with parts that go round and round to make air move
firework a thing with powder inside that makes colored lights and loud sounds when it burns
flood when there is a lot of water where it is usually dry
forest fire when trees burn in a large area of land that is covered with trees
forward going toward a place that's in front of you
fossil fuel things like coal or oil, that come from plants or animals that are millions of years old
fuel something that we use to produce heat or energy
gas a fossil fuel from under the ground; not a solid or a liquid; like air
gasoline a liquid that burns and powers an engine
generator a machine that makes electricity
global warming the way that Earth's temperature is getting higher
glow to make a small amount of light
greenhouse gas a gas that keeps Earth warm
grow to get bigger
hairdryer a machine that people use to make their hair dry
hole a space in something
ice frozen water
insulator a material that stops heat, electricity, or sound leaving something
invisible something that we can't see
keep to stay; to make something stay
kill to make someone or something die

kinetic energy that's moving
laser a strong type of light made by machines
liquid not a solid or a gas; like water
living thing something that lives; people, plants, and animals are living things
low not high
luminous something that produces light; lamps and candles are luminous
material something that we use to make other things
melt to become liquid because of being hot
metal a hard material made from minerals
miner a person who takes coal, metals, and other materials from under the ground
mixture different things together
molecule a very small thing that's made of two or more atoms
mud wet soil
non-renewable will run out
nuclear a type of energy that people use to make electricity
nucleus a part of an atom
oil a liquid fossil fuel from under the ground
oil rig a building that people use to take oil from the bottom of the ocean
opaque you can't see through it
operate to cut open someone; doctors operate to make sick people well
oven you cook food inside it
photovoltaic cell something that converts light into electricity
pipe a long, round thing that has a tunnel going through it
potential a type of energy that is stored
power to make something move or work
power station a building where electricity is made
problem something that is difficult
propeller a machine that turns quickly to power a ship or aircraft
push to make something move away
reduce to make something smaller or less
renewable will not run out

river water on land that goes to the ocean
roof the top part of a building
run out when there is no more of something because it is finished
shadow a dark, flat shape that something makes when it stops light
sky (*plural* **skies**) where the clouds and the sun are
solid hard; not liquid or gas
sound wave a movement of sound through air
space an area where there is nothing; where the moon and stars are
spark a very small piece of material that's burning
stir to move something around
store to keep something to use later
stretch to pull
temperature how hot or cold something is
toaster a machine that makes bread hot
transparent you can see through it
turbine a machine that is used to help make electricity
uranium a metal that is used to make nuclear energy
useful that helps someone to do something
vehicle something that moves things or people
vibrate to move very quickly up and down, or forward and backward
waste things that we throw away
well a hole that people make to take oil or water from the ground
wire a thin, metal string
without not having something; not doing something

Oxford Read and Discover

Series Editor: Hazel Geatches • CLIL Adviser: John Clegg

Oxford Read and Discover graded readers are at four levels, from 3 to 6, suitable for students from age 8 and older. They cover many topics within three subject areas, and can support English across the curriculum, or Content and Language Integrated Learning (CLIL).

Available for each reader:
- Audio CD Pack (book & audio CD)
- Activity Book

For Teacher's Notes & CLIL Guidance go to
www.oup.com/elt/teacher/readanddiscover

Subject Area / Level	The World of Science & Technology	The Natural World	The World of Arts & Social Studies
3 — 600 headwords	• How We Make Products • Sound and Music • Super Structures • Your Five Senses	• Amazing Minibeasts • Animals in the Air • Life in Rainforests • Wonderful Water	• Festivals Around the World • Free Time Around the World
4 — 750 headwords	• All About Plants • How to Stay Healthy • Machines Then and Now • Why We Recycle	• All About Desert Life • All About Ocean Life • Animals at Night • Incredible Earth	• Animals in Art • Wonders of the Past
5 — 900 headwords	• Materials to Products • Medicine Then and Now • Transportation Then and Now • Wild Weather	• All About Islands • Animal Life Cycles • Exploring Our World • Great Migrations	• Homes Around the World • Our World in Art
6 — 1,050 headwords	• Cells and Microbes • Clothes Then and Now • Incredible Energy • Your Amazing Body	• All About Space • Caring for Our Planet • Earth Then and Now • Wonderful Ecosystems	• Helping Around the World • Food Around the World

For younger students, **Dolphin Readers** Levels Starter, 1, and 2 are available.